LITTLE AND THE WHITE HORSE

Written by Neil and Ting Morris
Illustrated by Anna Clarke
Historical advisor Marion Wood

Hodder and Stoughton
London Sydney Auckland Toronto

Little Bear liked hearing of the Crow tribe's past adventures. He listened to chief Lone Dog more closely than ever when he told of the day Little Bear's father was killed by the Blackfoot enemy.

After his father's death, Little Bear had been trained by his grandfather. He learned to use his bow so that the arrow never missed its mark. 'One day you'll be a fine warrior like your father,' his grandfather said.

Growing up

Indian children learned skills by watching and imitating adults. Boys spent a lot of time learning how to fight and hunt. They were taught how to make and look after weapons.

Everything to do with the home was the responsibility of women, who made and owned the tipis. Girls were taught how to prepare, soften and sew buffalo skins to use for tipis, clothes, cooking pots and containers.

When Little Bear killed his first grizzly bear, his grandfather told him to eat a piece of its heart. 'This will give you the bear's strength,' he said.

He made Little Bear a necklace of the bear's claws to protect him in battle. But to become a warrior he had to wait for the great spirit to visit him.

Little Bear went into the mountains to wait for a sign from the great spirit. He stayed there for many days and nights without food or drink. At last in a dream he saw a white horse marked with a red hand.

Initiation

When Indian boys became men, they believed that special objects seen in visions would protect them. These magical objects—eagle heads, claws, wings, medicine dolls and oddly shaped stones— were kept in a medicine bag, which was often made of otter skin.

They washed away their childhood in a sweat lodge. This was made of willow branches covered with buffalo skins to make it airtight. Water was poured on to red-hot stones to make the lodge hot and steamy.

When he returned to the camp, the medicine-man told him what his dream meant. 'The horse you saw was your father's,' he said. 'The spirit calls you to avenge his death. You must make yourself a shield.'

When Little Bear heard that Lone Dog was planning to steal horses from a Blackfoot camp, he was eager to join his first raiding party.

The warriors left the Crow camp at daybreak. Those who were to guide and warn them of danger dressed themselves in wolf-skins.

It was a long way to the Blackfoot camp, and there were many rivers and streams to cross. All the time the raiders kept a good look-out for any sign of the enemy.

When they were near the Blackfoot camp, they left their horses in a well-hidden place. They would all meet here again after the raid. Quietly they slipped towards the enemy tipis.

Horses

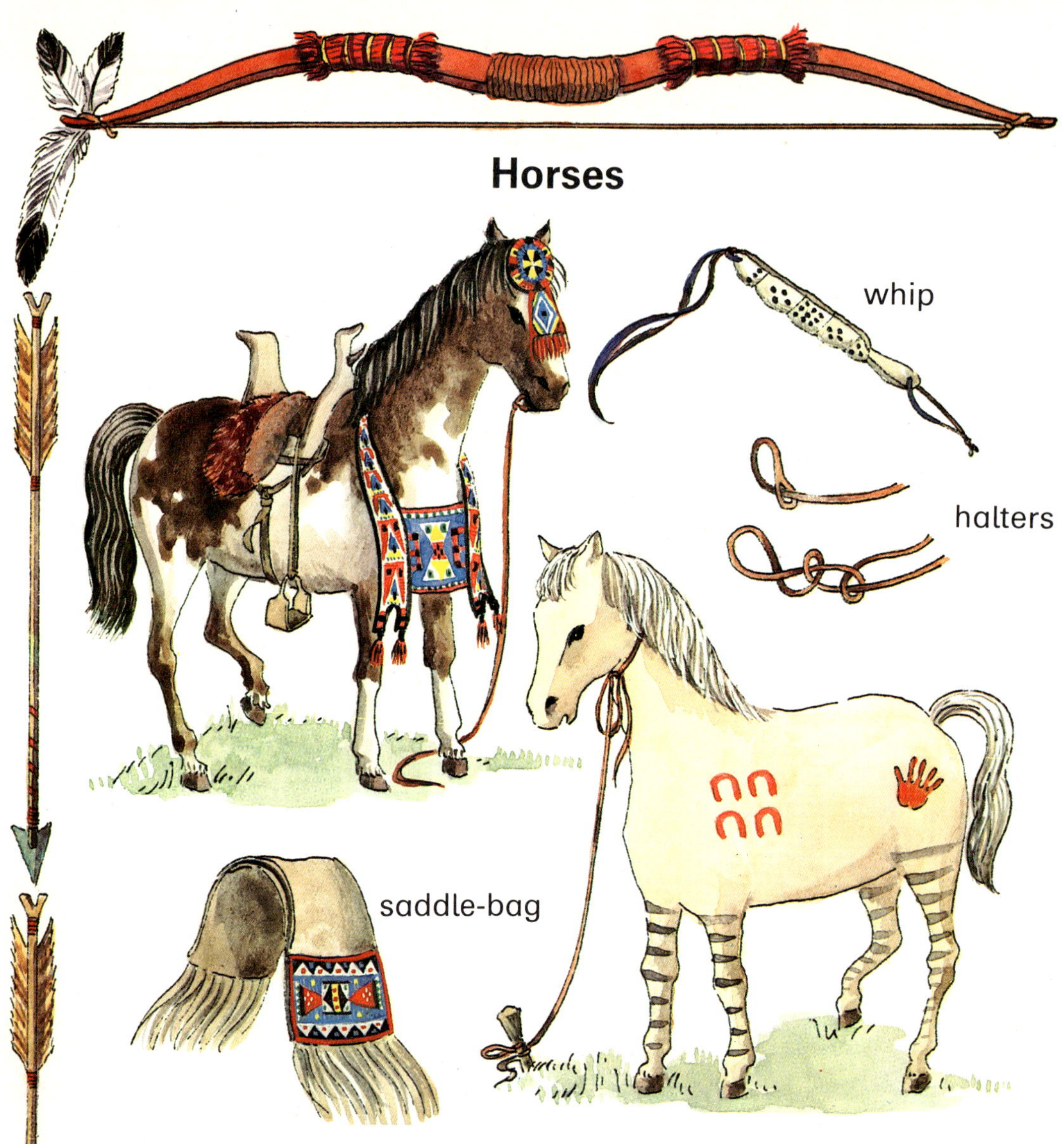

Before the Spaniards came to America 400 years ago, the Indians had never seen a horse. They got them from Spanish settlers by trading or stealing. The horse completely changed their lives, making travelling and hunting easier and battles more dangerous. It was their most valued possession, and stealing horses from another tribe was seen as a dangerous game and a way of showing courage. They painted symbols on their horses—a red hand showed that an enemy had been killed. Men usually rode bareback, while women had saddles made of wood, horn and rawhide.

Lone Dog led his warriors to a group of horses in the middle of the camp. Quickly they cut the ropes. Before they could be stopped, the warriors each jumped on a horse and galloped off.

As Little Bear went to cut another horse loose, he suddenly saw the white horse from his dream. It must be his father's!

He raced off on the white horse, but saw that two Blackfoot warriors were chasing him. They had heard the commotion and were eager for a fight.

Coups

Young Indians liked to measure their strength and courage against opponents from other tribes. The aim of many raids was not to kill, but to touch the enemy. Each touch, or coup, was made with the bare hand or with special coup sticks. These were decorated with paint, feathers and fur wrappings, and some were carved. All coup sticks were thought to have magical powers. Feathers were cut and coloured to show courage in battle; each design had a different meaning.

They chased Little Bear for miles, and he knew that he must stop and face them. He hid behind a tree and charged when they approached. He touched both warriors before overpowering them.

While they lay unconscious, Little Bear took their horses and medicine bundles. He was sure that the magic of the white horse had avenged his father.

When he reached the Crow hiding place, chief Lone Dog praised his skill and courage. He had beaten two Blackfoot and captured three horses!

Weapons and war objects

1 Scalp stretched on willow; Indians thought that by scalping enemies they would magically capture the dead man's strength. 2 Shield made from thick rawhide; the magic powers of the symbols gave special protection. 3 Wooden hoop decorated with medicine objects, used to protect groups of warriors. 4 Stone mace. 5 Knife, sheath and belt. 6 Tomahawk (battle hatchet). 7 Bow and arrows. 8 Lance.

The Crow warriors returned to their own camp in triumph. The raid had been a great success. Lone Dog led, as Little Bear proudly showed his newly won feathers.

Little Bear had proved his courage and was accepted into the council of warriors. At meetings he could now tell his own Crow adventure—of the day he recaptured his father's horse from the Blackfoot.